SPIRITUAL
INTERVIEW
WITH THE
GUARDIAN
SPIRIT OF

# ANGELA
# MERKEL

REVEALING HER TRUE
INTENTIONS, VISIONS,
AND CHALLENGES

RYUHO OKAWA

HS PRESS

# Contents

# *Preface*

On October 7, 2018, I gave an English lecture titled "Love for the Future" in Berlin, Germany. This book is the spiritual messages from the Guardian Spirit of Chancellor Merkel recorded in Tokyo about 10 days before the lecture with the aim of finding her real mind.

The basic way of thinking and mentality of Chancellor Merkel has been revealed through this book. Also, it clearly shows why her way of thinking conflicts with the American President Donald Trump.

I, myself, thought that Ms. Merkel was essentially a physicist from East Germany, but everything became clear to me after I found out that she was a great and honorable philosopher of Germany in her past life. The longest-reigning female chancellor-to-be and the de facto head of the EU is also a philosopher in a struggle between theory and practice.

In yesterday's news, Ms. Merkel announced her resignation as a party leader after losing twice in a row in regional elections. Her term as a chancellor lasts until fall 2021, so I just wish her the best of luck.

*Ryuho Okawa*
*Master & CEO of Happy Science Group*
*Oct. 30, 2018*

# Spiritual Interview with the Guardian Spirit of Angela Merkel

## Revealing Her True Intentions, Visions, and Challenges

Recorded September 28, 2018
Special Lecture Hall, Happy Science,
Japan

# Angela Merkel (1954 - Present)

A German politician born in West Germany. Moved to East Germany, a socialist country, after her father, a pastor, was offered a position at a church in East Berlin, where she then spent her early years. Merkel majored in physics at Karl Marx University, Leipzig (currently the University of Leipzig). After graduation, she went on to work at the Academy of Sciences, where she pursued her research in theoretical physics. Merkel took interest in politics after the fall of the Berlin Wall in 1989 and was successfully elected in the German federal election in 1990. She was appointed the leader of the Christian Democratic Union (CDU) in 2000. In 2005, Merkel became the chancellor of Germany; she is now serving her fourth term. She is the first female chancellor in German history. Merkel has been ranked first for seven consecutive years in "The World's 100 Most Powerful Women" list by Forbes.

Interviewers from Happy Science*:

## Masayuki Isono
Executive Director
Chief of Overseas Missionary Work Promotion Office
Deputy Chief Secretary, First Secretarial Division
Religious Affairs Headquarters

## Jiro Ayaori
Managing Director
Director General of Magazine Editing Division
Chief Editor of *The Liberty*
Lecturer at Happy Science University

## Hanako Cho
Deputy General Manager of Magazine Editing Division
Lecturer at Happy Science University

*No statements made by the guardian spirit of Ms. Merkel in this book reflect statements actually made by Ms. Merkel herself.*

*The opinions of the spirit do not necessarily reflect those of Happy Science Group. For the mechanism behind spiritual messages, see end section.*

---

# 1

## Inspiration of an Astonishing Spiritual Interview

**RYUHO OKAWA**

We'd like to challenge, "Spiritual Interview with the Guardian Spirit of Chancellor Merkel of Germany." She's the most powerful lady in the world, as you know. My inspiration says today will be an astonishing day, but you will know the conclusion at the end of this session. If you have enough power to converse with her, you are very respectable people, I think so.

To tell the truth, her guardian spirit can speak Japanese, but it's a secret. We must have a lesson speaking in English, so I'll never speak in Japanese [*laughs*]. I'll do my best, but she can understand Japanese. OK? Then, I'll call her.

[*Takes a deep breath.*]

Could I summon the guardian spirit of Angela Merkel? Could I summon the guardian spirit of Angela Merkel in Deutschland? The chancellor's guardian spirit, would you come down here? The guardian spirit of Angela Merkel.

[*About 12 seconds of silence.*]

# 2

# "My Aim is to Make One Organization for World Peace"

## ANGELA MERKEL'S GUARDIAN SPIRIT

Uh. *Guten Morgen* ("Good morning" in German).

## MASAYUKI ISONO

Guten Morgen. Are you the guardian spirit of Chancellor Merkel?

## MERKEL'S G.S.

Yeah.

## ISONO

Thank you very much for coming to Happy Science today. We are so happy to have you here. I'm so excited to have a talk with you. Thank you very much.

## MERKEL'S G.S.

Be cool.

**ISONO**

Be cool? Be good?

**MERKEL'S G.S.**

Cool. Cool.

**ISONO**

OK. Be cool.

**MERKEL'S G.S.**

Behave yourself.

**ISONO**

OK. Behave myself. OK. You became the first female chancellor in 2005. Since then, you have led Germany, the most powerful country of the EU, for these 13 years.

**MERKEL'S G.S.**

Thank you, thank you, thank you very much.

**ISONO**

I respect you so much. And you are well known as the most powerful lady in the world, so my first...

**MERKEL'S G.S.**

What is the meaning of "lady"?

**ISONO**

Lady? No, no, I just... [*Laughs.*]

**JIRO AYAORI**

Are you saying that you seem like a man... [*Laughs.*]

**MERKEL'S G.S.**

Most powerful "person."

**ISONO**

Person. I'm sorry. I made a mistake. So, you are the most powerful "leader" in the world.

**MERKEL'S G.S.**

OK. Better.

**ISONO**

OK. Thank you. So, my first question is, "What is the source of your leadership?"

**MERKEL'S G.S.**

*Denken* ("Think" in German). Ah. Think.

**ISONO**

To think.

**MERKEL'S G.S.**

Continue thinking.

**ISONO**

That...

**MERKEL'S G.S.**

And make good decisions. That's all.

**ISONO**

So, when you make decisions, what are the criteria or thinking you have?

## MERKEL'S G.S.

Firstly, study harder and harder. Next, listen to the opinions of famous people and then listen to the common people. And lastly, please listen to the voice of God and think within you. Obey your conscience and make a decision. OK?

## ISONO

Yes, Thank you very much.

## AYAORI

You said to listen to the voice of God. Could you tell us your viewpoint of faith?

## MERKEL'S G.S.

Viewpoint of faith? Formally, I'm a Christian. Formally. Traditional Christian.

## ISONO

OK.

**MERKEL'S G.S.**

In Germany.

**ISONO**

But...

**MERKEL'S G.S.**

"But"? But? No, it's a conclusion, so no.

**ISONO**

No?

**HANAKO CHO**

What kind of faith do you have right now?

**MERKEL'S G.S.**

I have faith in God. Large print God.

**ISONO**

G-O-D?

**MERKEL'S G.S.**

Oh, yeah.

**ISONO**

So, you believe in the Creator?

**MERKEL'S G.S.**

Yeah, not only Jesus Christ, but God. Printed in large "G."

**CHO**

Does it mean El Cantare?

**MERKEL'S G.S.**

You call him so, but it must be the conclusion, so never ask me too much.

**AYAORI**

OK. To be frank, your...

**MERKEL'S G.S.**

I can understand your English, so you can think in Japanese and speak poor English. OK?

**ISONO**

No, no, no, he's good at speaking English.

**MERKEL'S G.S.**

Really?

**ISONO**

Yes.

**MERKEL'S G.S.**

Sorry, sorry. I'm sorry.

**AYAORI**

It's OK. Thank you very much. Your approval rating...

**MERKEL'S G.S.**

I cannot understand your English.

## AYAORI

[*Laughs.*] Your...

## MERKEL'S G.S.

Your translation is very difficult. Is it Russian or...

## ISONO

No.

## AYAORI

...approval rating is...

## MERKEL'S G.S.

Ap, ap... appro?

## AYAORI

Approval.

## MERKEL'S G.S.

Approval?

**AYAORI**

Approval rating.

**MERKEL'S G.S.**

Approval rating?

**AYAORI**

Approval rating is falling...

**MERKEL'S G.S.**

Falling.

**AYAORI**

...now.

**MERKEL'S G.S.**

Fall in love?

**AYAORI**

No, no, no. "Falling." Sorry. Your political power is getting weaker.

**MERKEL'S G.S.**

Ah, I got it. You mean...

**AYAORI**

Sorry.

**MERKEL'S G.S.**

...fall down?

**AYAORI**

Yes. Yes.

**MERKEL'S G.S.**

My supporting rate...

**AYAORI**

Supporting rate.

**MERKEL'S G.S.**

Ah, I now understand. Your Japanese is very difficult, so... Sorry.

**AYAORI**

Your political power is getting weaker now.

**MERKEL'S G.S.**

Getting weaker... Oh, you're insulting me?

**AYAORI**

No, no, no, no. This situation is very severe for you. How do you see your political situation?

**MERKEL'S G.S.**

It's OK. I'm old enough. I'm 64. Now is the time I must leave this dirty world. I'll do my best to the end of my chancellor period, but I don't like this kind of dirty and too much emotional world of politics.* I studied a logical type of physics or things like that, so I don't like this dirty world.

---

* Weeks after this spiritual interview, Chancellor Merkel announced her resignation as the leader of CDU on October 29. She intends to continue her chancellorship until the end of the term in fall 2021, but will retire from politics after that.

## AYAORI

What is your goal as a politician or chancellor? What did you want to achieve as chancellor of Germany?

## MERKEL'S G.S.

My aim is to make the world one organization, for world peace, of course.

## AYAORI

One organization?

## MERKEL'S G.S.

Yeah, the EU is the first step. And the next step is a world organization more powerful than the United Nations as it is.

## AYAORI

That seems like totalitarianism.

**MERKEL'S G.S.**

Oh, no, no, not so. No, no, no, no. All countries are equal and independent, but they can argue about their serious problems in a common place, public place, and after their deliberately... they made... deliberately they make... hmm... furious, no, no, no... why is English so difficult... favorly, or... no, no, no... urgently... no, no... arguing... arguing very much, they can make a conclusion. At that time, they should obey the conclusion of the members. That is not totalitarianism, I think.

**CHO**

How do you view President Trump's recent speech at the United Nations? Because he stressed the importance of the sovereignty of each country many times.

**MERKEL'S G.S.**

Uh huh, he's a gunman, so he wants to do as he likes. He's threatening the world. It's his way of cowboy. In some meaning, such kind of person is required at the time of crisis, but in the usual period, we must have good conversations. I think so. He is too much self-concentrated person. I think so. If we can have more power, I mean the EU power, we can have an equal conversation with him, but he has a strong power, so it's difficult.

He's dividing the world now and he wants to go back to the age of wars, the war era of the Middle Age. I think so. Now is the day of democracy. He doesn't understand democracy. He just wants to be a champion. So, that's the problem.

## CHO
But Trump's position was to respect each country's independence. And they...

## MERKEL'S G.S.
No, no. It's a performance. No, no.

## CHO
He really wants each country to bear responsibility for their own prosperity.

## MERKEL'S G.S.

Yeah, yeah, yeah, it's true. It's true.

## CHO

I think that sounds reasonable. What do you think of his stance?

## MERKEL'S G.S.

All countries must be or should be equal, but the strengths, I mean the political strength, economic strength and the strength of leaders are quite different. All are not equal as it is.

So, we must have some kind of, how do I say, some kind of help for weaker countries, weaker leaders, and countries of poverty. He doesn't think about that. His "America-First" policy, in some meaning, will be successful for the American people, but in another meaning, it will destroy the world order. I think so.

# 3

# Views on Trump, Xi Jinping, and Putin

## ISONO

Now, you seem to have a severe attitude or severe stance toward President Trump of the United States. So, how can you manage the relationship between the United States and Germany or the EU?

## MERKEL'S G.S.

The United States, it's in New York, so they are under the control of the United... ah, the United Nations are under the control of the United States of America, so it's not neutral, I think. America's enemy is an enemy of the United Nations.

We need balance. The balance is, one is of course the United States and another one is of course the EU, and the third one might be the Asian power. The Asian power logically leads to the conclusion that it must be made by Japan and China. In the near future, the African power must be added to that.

## ISONO

How will you make a good relationship between the United States of America and the EU?

## MERKEL'S G.S.

Firstly, Mr. Donald Trump must learn that American law is not the world law or common law in the meaning of cosmopolitanism and international law. American law is not international law.

It's also the same for China. China's inner law is not international law. Xi Jinping doesn't understand this truth. Both Xi Jinping and Donald Trump, and adding to that, Russian Putin. He also cannot understand. Russian rule is the world rule, he thinks so. These dictatorships must have a chance to learn about the world; world geographic studying and the main rule of international law. They have *Defekt* ("flaw" in German) in that point. They don't have enough common law in them.

I said common law, it's an easy saying, but in another meaning, my common law is a law of conscience and of course the law of God. God is not assisting the United States only. God assists all the world, all the countries of the world, so Donald Trump can say instead of the American people the profit of the United States, but it's not enough. It's one part of the common law. Another common law is required to help other countries and other nations of other religions which they belong to. They are lacking. So, even if they have divine nature and charismatic personality, they are tribe-level gods, small "g" gods, I think so.

## ISONO

Thank you. Since you referred to the world leaders, could you tell us what you think of President Xi Jinping of China and President Putin of Russia?

## MERKEL'S G.S.

Xi Jinping is a difficult person, I think so. If you want to make him an enemy, it's easy to make him angry and that will make a new war in the near future. But he's very kind to his friends. He has two characters in him, so we need some kind of comprehension between Xi Jinping and us, the world leaders. He's a difficult person.

But if you study deep into the world history, number-one-China era covered almost half of the world, I think, especially in these 2,000 years. So, we must think that the age of China is coming in the near future, more than 50 percent level. We must stand that kind of age. But in another situation, we can control China under the name of the United Nations or under the name of relationship between the EU, Japan, the United States, and Russia, I think so.

And you added Vladimir Putin?

**ISONO**
Yes.

**MERKEL'S G.S.**
Ah, hmm. He's one of the dictators, I think. His dictatorship is very skillful, I think, so I appreciate him in his skill, but his understanding of democracy is maybe 50 percent or so. He must learn a lot from other democratic countries. He is from KGB, so he

has a very suspicious mind in him. He cannot rely on other countries. He is apt to think that they are enemies, so it's a problem. It's like China.

But I had several conversations with him and he's a very smart guy. He can think and he can make new rules by himself. So, the country Russia can be made in any direction if he wants. The importance is the intelligence which he gets from other leaders of the world, I think.

The isolation of Russia is not so good, I think. But we are now making economic sanctions with the United States, the EU, and Japan, so he's being isolated, but it's a not-so-good direction.

# 4

# Can We Change the Regime of China, A Country of No God?

## AYAORI

You said the United Nations and the United States, Japan, and the EU can control China. Does that mean we can change the Chinese regime?

## MERKEL'S G.S.

[*Clicks tongue.*] Ah, it's difficult. They lack the concept of God. That's a problem. Xi Jinping is God. Yeah, of course in our histories, God himself appeared in human history, but in the area of politics, it's very dangerous, I think so.

God who has human nature can be acceptable in our histories, but usually, he or she must be a strong leader in the mindset-changers meaning. The practical political power is not the condition of God and the existence of God's power itself. This political power must be made from the gathered power of people. I think so.

## AYAORI

What do you think of the oppression to religious groups in China, such as Christians and Muslims? What do you think of the violation of human rights in China?

## MERKEL'S G.S.

[*Sighs.*] It's difficult. Communist one-party system denies God and religion. They think of religion as LSD or a drug-like thing. In another meaning, they think of religion as a mind-controller, the spring of mind-controllers. So, religious leaders can mind-control their people and it will usually confront with political power and make confusion and conflict. That is the reason he doesn't like religions.

It's from the history of China. In the history of China, sometimes there occurred a political revolution, but in anytime, it occurred from religious leaders. This is their own conditions, so it's difficult to persuade him.

He is, for example, afraid of... how do you say... "Horinko" group (Falun Gong), or Christian groups of China. They have more than one hundred million population. It's over the communist members in China. It's difficult to deal with, so he is fearing religious groups. You, Happy Science will be next.

## AYAORI

Germany has been building a good economic relationship with China, but in a spiritual message from Jesus Christ...

## MERKEL'S G.S.

Jesus Christ. OK.

## AYAORI

...and in his message, he said, "Which do you like, money or God?"*

---

* On September 25, 2018, three days before this spiritual interview, the author conducted a Q&A session titled, "Jesus Christ's Answers In English" at Happy Science General Headquarters. It was a session where Jesus Christ answered questions in the form of a spiritual message. In the session, one of the interviewers asked Jesus about the strengthening economic ties between Germany and atheist China, to which he first replied, "Which do you like, money or God?"

**MERKEL'S G.S.**

Of course, money.

**AYAORI**

"Of course, money"? [*Laughs.*]

**MERKEL'S G.S.**

Yeah. God said, "Love poverty." So, he's evil.

**AYAORI**

But you said you believe in God.

**MERKEL'S G.S.**

Uh huh. Wealthy God is good. It's a meaning of Protestant, you know?

**ISONO**

It's true. It's true.

**MERKEL'S G.S.**

It's true.

## CHO

How do you see President Trump's policy of imposing tariffs on the Chinese economy? Because it seems that he wants to make the Chinese economy weaker in order to stop military expansion.

## MERKEL'S G.S.

Umm, the effect will be half and half. In some meaning, it has influence, of course, but in another meaning, it will make the people of the world poorer and poorer because they must pay more money to buy common things, like food, cars, other electronic tools, or something. So, it's not so good for people.

## ISONO

What do you think of President Xi Jinping's plan, "One Belt One Road" initiative?

## MERKEL'S G.S.

Hmm, it's his ambition. If he were a god, it will be a good policy. If he were a satan, it's not good.

Its "road" means his aim to make the countries surrender to him, the countries which are beside or on the belt or road. He wants to conquer these countries. If he were a satan, it's not good. If he were a god, it's a good thing. It depends. [*Laughs.*]

ISONO

Do you think President Xi is a god or a satan?

MERKEL'S G.S.

Maybe an ordinary person.

ISONO

Ordinary person?

MERKEL'S G.S.

Uh huh.

ISONO

Oh. So, you see President Xi as just an ordinary person.

## MERKEL'S G.S.

Ordinary person, but has a strength in will. Thinking-and-realizing-his-dream power is strong. It belongs to both god and satan.

## ISONO

Germany seems to support the Chinese plan, I mean, President Xi's One Belt One Road initiative. Am I correct?

## MERKEL'S G.S.

Yeah because he, or China, has been buying a lot of Mercedes-Benz. We got profit from China. So, we are not losing, we got money from China. But China will make inner-side economy to buy and sell the Mercedes-Benz and... I don't know about that. I have no concern about that. *Ich habe nichts zu tun* ("I have nothing to do" in German) about that. But as a country-to-country relationship, we made good profit. So, it's not so bad.

## AYAORI

Last year, Master Ryuho Okawa pointed out that it's possible that the EU and China will collapse at the same time.*

## MERKEL'S G.S.

Hahahaha, oh, no, no, no!

## AYAORI

What is your outlook?

## MERKEL'S G.S.

No, no. At the same time!?

## AYAORI

At the same time.

## MERKEL'S G.S.

Who wants to do that?

---

* On February 1, 2017, the author had mentioned the possible collapse of both the EU and China.

**AYAORI**

Uh...

**MERKEL'S G.S.**

Trump?

**AYAORI**

Yes, Trump is aiming to make the Chinese economy collapse.

**MERKEL'S G.S.**

He will fall in the next election.

**AYAORI**

What is your outlook about the Chinese economy?

**MERKEL'S G.S.**

Hmm... Now, they are in the situation of a trade war, I mean between the United States and China. Both will lose in the conclusion. So, I'm afraid the world economic recession will occur from this conflict. It can.

**ISONO**

You studied physics at university.

**MERKEL'S G.S.**

Ah, yeah.

**ISONO**

And some people criticize that you don't have much knowledge or understanding about economics.

**MERKEL'S G.S.**

Of course, that's right. That's right.

**ISONO**

Do you agree?

**MERKEL'S G.S.**

I agree. I don't have much concern about that. But I can read the figure only. It's black or red. OK. I can read the figures of the conclusion of the B/S (balance sheet).

**ISONO**

So, your basic or fundamental understanding of economics is black or red?

**MERKEL'S G.S.**

Yeah, that's right.

**ISONO**

Is that all?

**MERKEL'S G.S.**

Yeah. Yeah, my physical legal mind says so.

# 5

## Any Good Policies for
## The German Economy?

### CHO

Master Okawa said that unless Germany is strong in the EU, the EU will not prosper. So, I think the German economy is very important. Do you have any good economic policies?

### MERKEL'S G.S.

Oh, I'm too kind to weaker people. I have too much intention to rescue the refugees from Africa and Syria, and the Turkish people. So, they say that will make the German economy weaker and weaker. They say so. But I have conscience within me, so it's beyond economy. I must help them. I'm simply thinking that I get a lot of money from China and use it to help refugees. That's all. Very smart and simple.

**ISONO**

Yes. It's very simple.

**CHO**

But when an economic crisis happened... when the Greek debt crisis happened in 2010, your country didn't really help.

**MERKEL'S G.S.**

Oh, I'm a physicist, so at that time I will leave this position, so I have no problem.

**AYAORI**

You strongly insist on instituting an austerity policy on other countries in the EU. That makes negative impact...

**MERKEL'S G.S.**

Negative impact? What do you mean?

**AYAORI**

...on the EU economy.

## MERKEL'S G.S.

What do you mean by negative impact? I can't understand your English. What is negative impact?

## AYAORI

Many other countries don't have enough budget, so they can't manage their economy.

## MERKEL'S G.S.

But I say that every country like Greece—it's a small and weak economy they have—all of them must stand up by themselves. I said so. They said it's too cold or unfriendly, but I learned this philosophy from Master Ryuho Okawa, so it's correct, I think so.

## CHO

With regard to your immigrant policy, I learned recently that about one-fifth of the people in Germany are immigrants from other countries. So, that's why many right wing parties, such as AfD, Alternative für Deutschland, emerged, becoming powerful. What do you think of this kind of populist movement in Germany?

## MERKEL'S G.S.

Hmm. In some meaning, it was predictable. But I am the love of the world [*laughs*], so I must help weaker people. Master Okawa will come soon to Deutschland, oh, Germany*, and he will say the same thing. "To help the people of the world, the poor people, that is the mission of religion. So, Happy Science will supply a lot of money to Germany," he will say so. "I will bring a lot of money from Japan to Germany," he will say so, he must say so.

## CHO

I think one of the reasons your party's supporting rate is declining is because of your policy on immigrants. Do you think you have to reflect upon your immigrant policy in order to gain more power of your party?

---

* On October 7, 2018, the author held a lecture titled, "Love for the Future" and its Q&A session in English at The Ritz-Carlton, Berlin, Germany.

## MERKEL'S G.S.

Uh huh. To tell the truth, I, myself as a human, I like to live poor. It leads to the intellectual life, I think so. Gaining money too much makes people weaker in their brain thinking. So, too much money is a poison, I think so, in reality, in my heart.

## ISONO

Are you saying you hate wealth deep in your mind?

## MERKEL'S G.S.

In reality, I'm not a politician. I think like a physicist, so I don't like secular problems. Donald Trump is a very secular person, you know? He is good at earning money and using money and playing with girls, like that, buy land and sell land and build buildings and sell them. He is good at these kinds of secular matters. But to tell the truth, I don't like those kinds of matters. I just want to think.

# 6

# Where Did Nazism Come From?

**ISONO**

OK. You mentioned that you have conscience. So, you want to help poor people.

**MERKEL'S G.S.**

Yeah.

**ISONO**

Is it related to the German history, I mean Nazism?

**MERKEL'S G.S.**

Oh, I'm quite contrary to Nazism. I hate it. I hate Nietzscheism, I hate Heidegger, and I also hate Hegelian. These kinds of thoughts have made totalitarian system or supported totalitarian system. You usually say, "It's a mistake of Karl Marx," but it's from Hegelian philosophy. Next were Nietzsche and Heidegger.

So, German philosophies made totalitarianism and Hegel's godlike philosophy produced the chosen-people thought in Germany and it made anti-Semitism, I mean the anti-Jewish people-ism. Anti-Semitism comes from this kind of Hegelian and Nietzschean thoughts. I think so.

## CHO

Is there any philosopher you admire?

## MERKEL'S G.S.

Hmm. Buddha is not so bad. He is not a philosopher, but it's not so bad. Jesus Christ has a problem, of course. If he lived in these days, he would be a refugee, Turkish people- or Syrian people- or Egyptian people- or Libyan people-like person, maybe. No goods, no money, and beg for food.

## ISONO

I think Germany is prosperous in the economic meaning, but Germany doesn't have a central pole in mentality or philosophy. What kind of philosophy or thinking idea...

## MERKEL'S G.S.

No, no. We don't need such kind of central pole. From the starting point, Martin Luther of Protestantism said, "Don't belong to churches. Don't belong to the Roman Catholic or one Pope. You, yourself belong to God through reading the German translation of the New Testament. Please read the German-translated New Testament and belong to God by oneself, in each family." That is the starting point of our religion, so everyone is independent in this meaning. We don't need "one-pole system"-like thinking.

# 7

## "My Dream in the Next Century is 'A Global-Level Government'"

**AYAORI**

What kind of vision do you have for the future of the EU or Germany?

**MERKEL'S G.S.**

To tell the truth, I'm not so strong at building new economy. I was born in West Germany, but brought up in East Germany. So I, myself suffered a lot of influence from the old-fashioned Russian style of politics and economy. So, it's very difficult. I'm not a Donald Trump-like person, so I am not so good at selling and buying. Before me, there was Margaret Thatcher in the U.K. She was good at buying and selling because she was a girl of a small store, but I am not.

So, I have a dream and a theory, but it's very pure and so people cannot follow me, I think so. But my dream will come true in the next century. I hope so.

## CHO
What is your dream?

## MERKEL'S G.S.
"Gather a lot of nations and have conversations and make decisions and follow them. And every country, every nation is equal, but they all believe in God and hate war" system is essential. I think so.

## AYAORI
Who will be your God at that time?

## MERKEL'S G.S.
Oh. The God of the Earth [see Figure 1].

## AYAORI
So, you mean we should have one government in the next century?

## MERKEL'S G.S.

Hmm, that expression is misleading, so... We must think about a global-level government. It's not the one-party system of communists. It's quite different. We need conversations. We must reflect a lot of opinions from other countries.

But the problem is, if one country has one vote, the weaker countries have a lot of members, so in the economic meaning, it is unprofitable for stronger countries in economy like Japan or the United States or the U.K. or Germany or France, like those countries.

 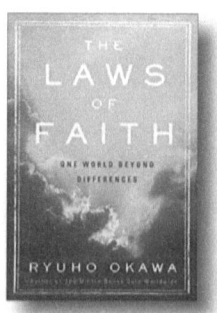

Figure 1.
Happy Science has revealed the existence of El Cantare, God of the Earth, who was involved in the creation of humans on Earth and holds the highest authority on Earth. See *The Laws of the Sun* and *The Laws of Faith* (both by Ryuho Okawa [New York: IRH Press, 2018]).

## AYAORI

Do you mean the United Nations will transform into a world government?

## MERKEL'S G.S.

Hmm, it would be one possibility. But to tell the truth, the United Nations lacks the budget and the leaders of first level, or topflight leaders because the leader of the United Nations is selected from third countries, I mean not great countries, for example, South Korea. Not the president or the prime minister, but the foreign minister-level people will be elected. So, their management power is not so high. It's a problem. The American president usually looks down upon the secretary-general of the United Nations. Maybe he or she will come from the weak countries, a foreign minister-level person.

## CHO

What do you think of the concept of sovereignty? Because Brexit happened: many British people wanted to make their country's decisions on their own. That's really the issue here.

## MERKEL'S G.S.

It's not so good. It's isolationism and a self-concentrated thinking like Donald Trump's. They are keeping their own money. They are afraid of getting rid of their money, from them to weaker countries of the EU or other countries of Africa or Islamic countries.

So, the United Kingdom is running away from the EU with their money. But it means too much burden on Germany and France. It's a beginning of the collapse of the EU. I think so.

## CHO

So, you mean the concept of sovereignty or nationalism is not important anymore?

## MERKEL'S G.S.

Hmm, in some meaning, it's important. Sovereignty or nationality is important. Managing the EU is very difficult. I have been feeling difficulties in many languages and of course the traditions and cultures of every nation. So, from the beginning it was forecast to be very difficult.

But we must resist against this kind of confusion. We must conquer this confusion. We can learn from each other. The German people, to tell the truth, don't like the French people, and of course the U.K. people, the United States people, and the Russian people and, in addition to that, they don't like the Japanese people. These are strong countries in economy, and of course, in the military meaning. So, we cannot sleep well if they were getting stronger and stronger.

## CHO

But due to the globalization, your country also lost jobs. The gap between the haves and have-nots is increasing in Germany as well. So, what do you think of this situation in Germany?

## MERKEL'S G.S.

Oh, at that time, I want to study physics and reading books and hiking and have fun listening to classical music. I worked a lot. It's enough. So, it's the next person who carries the burden from other countries. It's beyond my power.

# 8

# What Merkel's Guardian Spirit Thinks of National Security

**ISONO**

I would like to ask you about your view of military power.

**MERKEL'S G.S.**

Military power?

**ISONO**

Since you hate war, you don't want war...

**MERKEL'S G.S.**

Oh.

**ISONO**

Of course, we don't want war, but some people said, "We can stop war because we have defensive power." Do you agree with it?

## MERKEL'S G.S.

In the theoretical thinking, if the United States abandons budget for their arms, it will help the poverty of all over the world. They can. But at the same time, there needs the abandonment of armed forces of China and Russia. At that time, if Russia abandoned that kind of arming budget, the EU can reduce such kind of budget and these budgets can be used for the purpose of helping poor people of the world.

Almost billions of people are lacking food every day, so we can help them. We will teach them, for example the African people, the technology for peacemaking and how they can make their own revenue of the nation and budget. At that time we want to say to them, "Be independent." So, military budget reduction, I mean, make it fewer and fewer is essential for the time being, I think.

## ISONO

How can you persuade the world leaders to abandon their military power?

## MERKEL'S G.S.

The bottleneck is Hitler's thing. We can't say too much about that. They, meaning the countries surrounding us, usually say, "You are the most dangerous country." They say so. "You produced Adolf Hitler and destroyed the world," so we don't have enough opinion about that. We are in the same situation like Japan in this meaning. But now is the day to reconsider about that. Adolf Hitler was born in Austria, so [*laughs*] it's not Germany.

## AYAORI

But President Trump is proposing that Germany should increase its military budget to two to four percent of the GDP. What do you think of that proposal?

## MERKEL'S G.S.

Donald Trump is good at thinking money, so I hate him. We don't need any money for defending our country. Love peace and love God. That's cheap.

## ISONO

But I think the Western countries fear Russia because Russia was their enemy in the Cold War, so...

## MERKEL'S G.S.

Yeah, enemy. Yeah, indeed enemy.

## ISONO

So, if you want to protect your country and the EU, I think you need NATO. But you don't want to support the NATO system?

## MERKEL'S G.S.

Ah, the NATO system [*clicks tongue*]. It costs a lot.

## ISONO

Yes, it does.

## MERKEL'S G.S.

Main target is Russia, so [*clicks tongue*] it's difficult. Russia has a lot of nuclear weapons, so NATO must protect themselves from Russia.

We chose China to earn money and to make a balance between Russia and the EU. If we have a good relationship with China, then the EU and China can protect us from Russia.

## ISONO
Perhaps, are you thinking that the EU and China will have an alliance between them?

## MERKEL'S G.S.
China is far from Europe, so we don't think it's dangerous. But Russia did a lot to the EU, European countries. Sometimes Napoleon attacked Russia, but was ruined. Hitler attacked Russia, but was ruined. They are strong and in every time, they have been enemies of Europe. They have an expansionist idea. They need non-frozen sea, that's the reason, I think so. Give your northern islands to them, including Hokkaido. They will be happy. They can use the ocean.

# 9

## Views on Confucianism and Prime Minister Abe

**CHO**

With regard to the military threat of China, although China is located far away from Europe, actually, German companies' technologies are being stolen by Chinese companies.

**MERKEL'S G.S.**

Yeah, that's true. That's true.

**CHO**

Don't you think that's a threat?

**MERKEL'S G.S.**

They buy Mercedes-Benz, so we are refunded enough.

**ISONO**

But they stole your intellectual properties.

**MERKEL'S G.S.**

Yeah, true.

**ISONO**

What do you think of that?

**MERKEL'S G.S.**

In some meaning, Donald Trump is correct in that meaning. Xi Jinping or the Chinese people don't understand that they are stealing. They say, "All the countries of the world have been stealing from China. Every invention of China, they stole."

**AYAORI**

Papers and...

**MERKEL'S G.S.**

Yeah, yeah, papers and black powder...

## ISONO

For making fire?

## MERKEL'S G.S.

Yeah, yeah. Fire and a lot of philosophies or like that. "China has been stolen," they say like that. "Europe is underdeveloped countries. Japan also." They say like that. "America is a new country, only 200 or 300 years. China has a 5,000-year history." They say so. They have China-concentrated thinking, so in some meaning, partly yes in true history. Yeah. China is a great country. They can confront Europe enough in the cultural meaning and of course, a lot of meanings. They look down upon Japan like that. From the viewpoint of China, Japan is like the Crete Island or Greek-like country in the EU.

## ISONO

Do you like Japan?

## MERKEL'S G.S.

Yeah, yeah. Partly yes.

## ISONO

Partly yes? [*Laughs.*]

## CHO

What do you think of the Confucius Institute* in your country? I think you have many. Like in Japan and in the U.S. This kind of ideological infiltration in your country, matters...

## MERKEL'S G.S.

Confucian thought is not a philosophy. It's a teaching, just a teaching. You can learn and learn by heart and understand and just use it. But the German philosophy is thinking, individual thinking. It depends on individual thinking, so it's a little different.

Even Confucianism, you think it's a good one, and you want to ask Xi Jinping to learn Confucianism instead of Sonshi (Sun-Tzu) or that

---

* An educational institute that was founded by the Chinese government in 2004 in order to promote the Chinese language and culture. The institute has locations around the world, many of them operating on university campuses. There are over 500 locations in about 140 countries (as of December 2016). Some people say the institute is propagating philosophies of the Communist Party of China as well as engaging in espionage.

kind of war philosophy, but even Confucianism is a totalitarian attitude. It is a managing system and it builds the nation in one theory. So, it's not so democratic, I think.

## AYAORI

How do you evaluate Prime Minister Abe?

## MERKEL'S G.S.

Prime Minster Abe? Hmm, he's famous because of his long-reigning period. Usually, the Japanese prime minister will change year by year, so no one can understand or remember their names, but Mr. Abe is famous.

It's good for you, but he's not so popular in the EU. He just looks at the United States only. And in my opinion, he is aiming at realizing the re-militarization of Japan. He is possessed by ghosts of Japanese empire army. Maybe.

# 10

## Merkel's Past Life—a Great Philosopher Who Sought for Perpetual Peace

**ISONO**

I'd like to ask you about your spiritual secret.

**MERKEL'S G.S.**

Oh. Spiritual secret. Hum.

**ISONO**

Before this session began, Master Okawa said "today will be an astonishing day."

**MERKEL'S G.S.**

Uh huh. Yeah.

**ISONO**

What do you think he means?

**MERKEL'S G.S.**

Hmm. It means I'm not she, I'm not he. I'm human.

**ISONO**

That means you are an existence beyond the sexes or genders?

**MERKEL'S G.S.**

No, no, no.

**ISONO**

What do you mean?

**MERKEL'S G.S.**

Hahahaha. Yeah, Angela Merkel is a lady now. But her guardian spirit is a man.

**ISONO**

So, you are a male.

**MERKEL'S G.S.**

Yeah, male.

## ISONO

If possible, could you reveal your name, please?

## MERKEL'S G.S.

Oh, you know. You know my name, of course. All the Japanese know my name.

## ISONO

Could you give us a tip or hint? In which era?

## MERKEL'S G.S.

I'm a philosopher.

## CHO

Kant?

## MERKEL'S G.S.

Ah, Immanuel Kant*. So, I'm not so good at economy. You know?

---

* Immanuel Kant (1724-1804) was a German philosopher. He advocated critical philosophy through his three works, *Critique of Pure Reason*, *Critique of Practical Reason*, and *Critique of Judgment*. Kant is considered the father of German idealism and gave great influence on the later Western philosophy. The ideas in his book Perpetual Peace influenced the establishment of the League of Nations.

## ISONO

So, Immanuel Kant is reborn as Chancellor Angela Merkel.

## MERKEL'S G.S.

Yeah, true.

## ISONO

Yeah, it's an astonishing fact. It is.

## MERKEL'S G.S.

Yeah. Your Master predicted so. I have already published my spiritual books... [See Figure 2.]

## ISONO

Yes. Spiritual message.

Figure 2.
Kant has been a supporting spirit since the early days of Happy Science. Happy Science has published four books of spiritual messages by Kant in Japanese, one of which is translated into English. See Ryuho Okawa, *Critique of Current World Affairs: Immanuel Kant's advice from Heaven* (Tokyo: Happy Science, 2016).

## MERKEL'S G.S.

...in your group. So, I also am a guiding spirit of Happy Science.

## ISONO

Ah, I see. Master said you can speak Japanese, too.

## MERKEL'S G.S.

Yeah, of course.

## ISONO

So, that means...

## MERKEL'S G.S.

*Hanaseruyo* ("I can speak" in Japanese), of course.

## ISONO

[*Laughs.*] No, please speak in English this time.

## MERKEL'S G.S.

I'm *hikari no tenshi ne. Dakara nihongo shabereru ne* ("an angel of light, so I can speak Japanese" in Japanese).

[*Interviewers and audience laugh.*]

## MERKEL'S G.S.

I can speak Japanese because I'm an angel of light.

## ISONO

That means you once were a Japanese? You were once born in Japan? Is it...

## MERKEL'S G.S.

In Japan? Hmm... No, I'm a European, I have been. But Japanese people learned a lot from me.

## ISONO

Yes. We studied...

## MERKEL'S G.S.

Yeah, Meiji period, Taisho period, and Showa period. And now nothing to learn from me.

## AYAORI

Your purpose of being born in this age is to make peace in Europe?

## MERKEL'S G.S.

I am the origin of the thinking to build up the United Nations, and the small United Nations is the EU, so I appeared.

## AYAORI

You want a world government in the next century?

## MERKEL'S G.S.

Yeah, a Kant-like government. We are confronted with the issue of China. You dislike China and have a containing-China policy. But I have an idea of how to steal from China in terms of money. So, we are Dracula to get blood from China.

## ISONO

So now, Germany is stealing wealth from China?

## MERKEL'S G.S.

Yeah, yeah. Today, they want Mercedes-Benz or Germans' very developed technologies or goods, so they admire Germany. But it will make them modernized and westernized. And at the tipping point, they will change.

Karl Marx is not a good German, but his influence is still in China. So, they have respect for Germany. Their political thinking is from Karl Marx, so we will change China at the tipping point. So, never mind. I can, we can change China.

Japan already studied Kant's philosophy. It's old-fashion now, but it's really made modern Japanese thinking methods, so at that time, Japan can be a leader of China.

## AYAORI

I think President Trump and Chancellor Merkel can cooperate with each other. That will make the world prosperous and peaceful.

## MERKEL'S G.S.

He is a man of sex, but I am a man of philosophy.

**ISONO**

But President Trump was President George Washington, the first president, in one of his past lives [see Figure 3].

**MERKEL'S G.S.**

Really? Oh, really? He's a very poor farmer.

**ISONO**

[*Laughs.*] Yes, but President Trump helps Lord El Cantare's ideas and plans, so please help him and...

**MERKEL'S G.S.**

Ah, he should study more. He cannot understand Kant's philosophy, so he needs more talented brain. He must be reborn again.

Figure 3.
Spiritual investigations by Happy Science have revealed that President Trump was George Washington in his past life. See Chapters 3 and 4 in Ryuho Okawa, *The Trump Secret: Seeing Through the Past, Present, and Future of the New American President* (New York: IRH Press, 2017).

## AYAORI

If you want to be in power for a few more years, you should cooperate with him.

## MERKEL'S G.S.

I know. Of course, I can be the teacher of Donald Trump, but he will not hear me. He's a bad student, so he never will.

## ISONO OK.

The time is almost up, so lastly, could you give a message to the people of Germany and the EU?

## MERKEL'S G.S.

Oh, OK. [*Sighs.*] Please remember. You, modern Japanese people owe a lot from Germany and now is the time to return it to Germany. Thank you very much. [*Laughs.*]

## ISONO

OK, thank you very much.

## MERKEL'S G.S.

*Mou iika ne*? ("Is that enough?" in Japanese.)

[*Audience laugh.*]

## MERKEL'S G.S.

*Mou, eigo wa tsukareru wa* ("It's tiresome to speak in English" in Japanese.) *Mou iika ne*? OK?

## ISONO

*Yoroshii desu ka? Hai. Saigo ni, sousai sensei ga kondo doitsu ni ikaremasu keredomo, nanika, ossharitaikoto toka arimasuka*? ("Is that OK? OK. Lastly, Master is going to Germany, so do you have anything to say to him?" in Japanese.)

## MERKEL'S G.S.

Please praise Angela Merkel. "She is the greatest lady in the world, this century." If your Master said so, it's enough.

## ISONO

OK, thank you very much.

## MERKEL'S G.S.

Thank you. [*Claps once.*]

## AYAORI

Thank you very much.

## MERKEL'S G.S.

Bye.

# 11

# After the Spiritual Interview

(Hereafter, the session was conducted in Japanese. The English text is a translation.)

## RYUHO OKAWA

So, that's the truth. I knew it was him, but he didn't tell us until the end.

I'm a bit shocked, too. When I talked to the guardian spirit in the dressing room beforehand, I asked him, "Can you speak Japanese?" "Yes." "Who are you?" He said, "Kant." I was surprised. But I needed to do a spiritual interview with Merkel, not Kant, because we already released a spiritual interview with Kant. I couldn't really let this session be about him.

I don't think she's very good at politics that are deeply involved with actual daily life. She's from East Germany, and communism is theoretical in a way, so someone who thinks like a physicist would be able to wrap their brain around it. She's probably somewhat suited for that. I believe she still has such a way of thinking. I don't think she's too fond of Trump's alchemist-like ability to turn anything into money.

Kant was a lonely philosopher, so it might be hard for him. I'm sure Merkel's life had been a tough trial. The idea at the root of the League of Nations came from Kant. It was based on his book, Perpetual Peace. But in reality, the League of Nations failed. Its successor, the UN, is not working well enough. Then, there came the EU, but things are quite difficult. I guess she's being put through both theory and practice.

Her ambitions are good, I guess, but there are many more difficulties in reality. It's hard for things to work out well when you have a couple dozen countries together that speak different languages. Being controlled by something like the government in Brussels is quite discouraging.

A while ago, someone mentioned that it was like having Kobe govern all of Japan. Kobe is better because it might actually be more like Oita. It's difficult to come up with an idea for all countries. They have problems like that. Ideals need to be pursued as ideals, but in reality, it's not so easy to get the nearly 200 countries in the world all together on the same page.

I don't know whether this spiritual interview will be published or not. She might have already quit by the time she gains confidence [*laughs*], but I would be happy if she were to leave us with some lessons to learn from.

We currently have different opinions on how to handle China. I guess, for Germany, China isn't so dangerous. They can't imagine China launching missiles at them. But Russia might. That's what they think. Our views differ on this, so we must work out what we have to do from now on.

But it's good that such a great empress appeared. There might be a successor to bring prosperity to Germany. [*Claps twice*] OK.

# ABOUT THE AUTHOR

Founder and CEO of Happy Science Group.

Ryuho Okawa was born on July 7th 1956, in Tokushima, Japan. After graduating from the University of Tokyo with a law degree, he joined a Tokyo-based trading house. While working at its New York headquarters, he studied international finance at the Graduate Center of the City University of New York. In 1981, he attained Great Enlightenment and became aware that he is El Cantare with a mission to bring salvation to all humankind.

In 1986, he established Happy Science. It now has members in over 165 countries across the world, with more than 700 branches and temples as well as 10,000 missionary houses around the world.

He has given over 3,400 lectures (of which more than 150 are in English) and published over 3,000 books (of which more than 600 are Spiritual Interview Series), and many are translated into 40 languages. Along with *The Laws of the Sun* and *The Laws Of Messiah*, many of the books have become best sellers or million sellers. To date, Happy Science has produced 25 movies. The original story and original concept were given by the Executive Producer Ryuho Okawa. He has also composed music and written lyrics of over 450 pieces.

Moreover, he is the Founder of Happy Science University and Happy Science Academy (Junior and Senior High School), Founder and President of the Happiness Realization Party, Founder and Honorary Headmaster of Happy Science Institute of Government and Management, Founder of IRH Press Co., Ltd., and the Chairperson of NEW STAR PRODUCTION Co., Ltd. and ARI Production Co., Ltd.

# WHAT IS EL CANTARE?

El Cantare means "the Light of the Earth," and is the Supreme God of the Earth who has been guiding humankind since the beginning of Genesis. He is whom Jesus called Father and Muhammad called Allah, and is *Ame-no-Mioya-Gami*, Japanese Father God. Different parts of El Cantare's core consciousness have descended to Earth in the past, once as Alpha and another as Elohim. His branch spirits, such as Shakyamuni Buddha and Hermes, have descended to Earth many times and helped to flourish many civilizations. To unite various religions and to integrate various fields of study in order to build a new civilization on Earth, a part of the core consciousness has descended to Earth as Master Ryuho Okawa.

**Alpha** is a part of the core consciousness of El Cantare who descended to Earth around 330 million years ago. Alpha preached Earth's Truths to harmonize and unify Earth-born humans and space people who came from other planets.

**Elohim** is a part of El Cantare's core consciousness who descended to Earth around 150 million years ago. He gave wisdom, mainly on the differences of light and darkness, good and evil.

**Ame-no-Mioya-Gami (Japanese Father God)** is the Creator God and the Father God who appears in the ancient literature, *Hotsuma Tsutae*. It is believed that He descended on the foothills of Mt. Fuji about 30,000 years ago and built the Fuji dynasty, which is the root of the Japanese civilization. With justice as the central pillar, Ame-no-Mioya-Gami's teachings spread to ancient civilizations of other countries in the world.

**Shakyamuni Buddha** was born as a prince into the Shakya Clan in India around 2,600 years ago. When he was 29 years old, he renounced the world and sought enlightenment. He later attained Great Enlightenment and founded Buddhism.

**Hermes** is one of the 12 Olympian gods in Greek mythology, but the spiritual Truth is that he taught the teachings of love and progress around 4,300 years ago that became the origin of the current Western civilization. He is a hero that truly existed.

**Ophealis** was born in Greece around 6,500 years ago and was the leader who took an expedition to as far as Egypt. He is the God of miracles, prosperity, and arts, and is known as Osiris in the Egyptian mythology.

**Rient Arl Croud** was born as a king of the ancient Incan Empire around 7,000 years ago and taught about the mysteries of the mind. In the heavenly world, he is responsible for the interactions that take place between various planets.

**Thoth** was an almighty leader who built the golden age of the Atlantic civilization around 12,000 years ago. In the Egyptian mythology, he is known as god Thoth.

**Ra Mu** was a leader who built the golden age of the civilization of Mu around 17,000 years ago. As a religious leader and a politician, he ruled by uniting religion and politics.

# WHAT IS A SPIRITUAL MESSAGE?

We are all spiritual beings living on this earth. The following is the mechanism behind Master Ryuho Okawa's spiritual messages.

## 1 You are a spirit

People are born into this world to gain wisdom through various experiences and return to the other world when their lives end. We are all spirits and repeat this cycle in order to refine our souls.

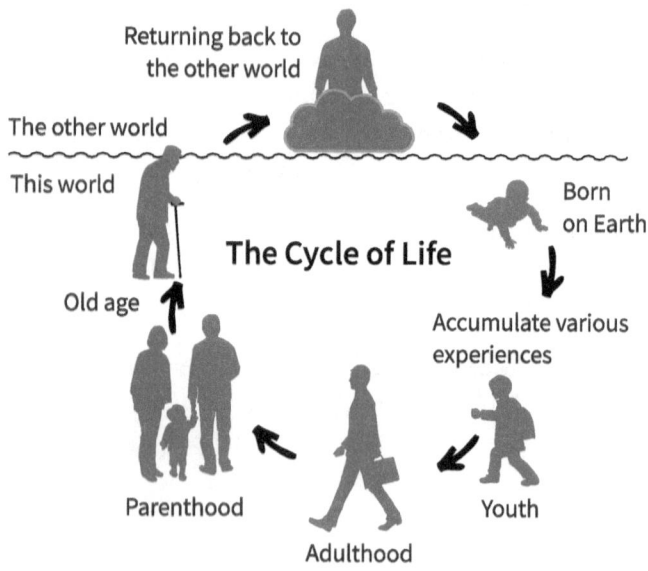

Returning back to the other world

The other world

This world

Old age

The Cycle of Life

Born on Earth

Accumulate various experiences

Parenthood

Adulthood

Youth

## 2 You have a guardian spirit

Guardian spirits are those who protect the people who are living on this earth. Each of us has a guardian spirit that watches over us and guides us from the other world. They were us in our past life, and are identical in how we think.

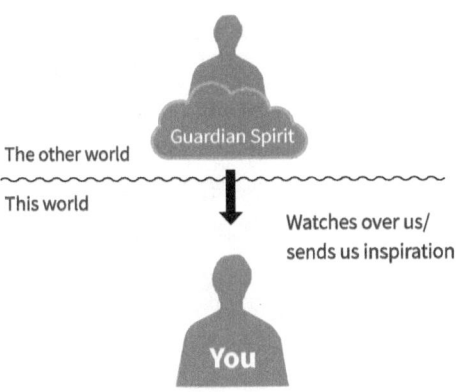

## 3 How spiritual messages work

Master Ryuho Okawa, through his enlightenment, is capable of summoning any spirit from anywhere in the world, including the spirit world.

Master Okawa's way of receiving spiritual messages is fundamentally different from that of other psychic mediums who undergo trances and are thereby completely taken over by the spirits they are channeling.

Master Okawa's attainment of a high level of enlightenment enables him to retain full control of his consciousness and body throughout the duration of the spiritual message. To allow the spirits to express their own thoughts and personalities freely, however, Master Okawa usually softens the dominancy of his consciousness. This way, he is able to keep his own philosophies out of the way and ensure that the spiritual messages are pure expressions of the spirits he is channeling.

Since guardian spirits think at the same subconscious level as the person living on earth, Master Okawa can summon the spirit and find out what the person on earth is actually thinking. If the person has already returned to the other world, the spirit can give messages to the people living on earth through Master Okawa.

Since 2009, many spiritual messages have been openly recorded by Master Okawa and published. Spiritual messages from the guardian spirits of people living today such as Donald Trump, former Japanese Prime Minister Shinzo Abe and Chinese President Xi Jinping, as well as spiritual messages sent from the spirit world by Jesus Christ, Muhammad, Thomas Edison, Mother Teresa, Steve Jobs and Nelson Mandela are just a tiny pack of spiritual messages that were published so far.

Domestically, in Japan, these spiritual messages are being read by a wide range of politicians and mass media, and the high-level contents of these books are delivering an impact even more on politics, news and public opinion. In recent years, there have been spiritual messages recorded in English, and

English translations are being done on the spiritual messages given in Japanese. These have been published overseas, one after another, and have started to shake the world.

1 The guardian spirit /
spirit in the other world...

2 Goes inside Master Okawa
in this world

3 Master Okawa speaks
the words of the guardian spirit /
spirit

*For more about spiritual messages and a complete list of books in the Spiritual Interview Series, visit <u>okawabooks.com</u>*

# ABOUT HAPPY SCIENCE

Happy Science is a global movement that empowers individuals to find purpose and spiritual happiness and to share that happiness with their families, societies, and the world. With more than 12 million members around the world, Happy Science aims to increase awareness of spiritual truths and expand our capacity for love, compassion, and joy so that together we can create the kind of world we all wish to live in.

Activities at Happy Science are based on the Principle of Happiness (Love, Wisdom, Self-Reflection, and Progress). This principle embraces worldwide philosophies and beliefs, transcending boundaries of culture and religions.

**Love** teaches us to give ourselves freely without expecting anything in return; it encompasses giving, nurturing, and forgiving.

**Wisdom** leads us to the insights of spiritual truths, and opens us to the true meaning of life and the will of God (the universe, the highest power, Buddha).

**Self-Reflection** brings a mindful, nonjudgmental lens to our thoughts and actions to help us find our truest selves—the essence of our souls—and deepen our connection to the highest power. It helps us attain a clean and peaceful mind and leads us to the right life path.

**Progress** emphasizes the positive, dynamic aspects of our spiritual growth—actions we can take to manifest and spread happiness around the world. It's a path that not only expands our soul growth, but also furthers the collective potential of the world we live in.

## PROGRAMS AND EVENTS

The doors of Happy Science are open to all. We offer a variety of programs and events, including self-exploration and self-growth programs, spiritual seminars, meditation and contemplation sessions, study groups, and book events.

Our programs are designed to:
* Deepen your understanding of your purpose and meaning in life
* Improve your relationships and increase your capacity to love unconditionally
* Attain peace of mind, decrease anxiety and stress, and feel positive
* Gain deeper insights and a broader perspective on the world
* Learn how to overcome life's challenges
  ... and much more.

*For more information, visit <u>happy-science.org</u>.*

# CONTACT INFORMATION

Happy Science is a worldwide organization with branches and temples around the globe. For a comprehensive list, visit the worldwide directory at *happy-science.org*. The following are some of the many Happy Science locations:

## UNITED STATES AND CANADA

### New York
79 Franklin St., New York, NY 10013, USA
Phone: 1-212-343-7972
Fax: 1-212-343-7973
Email: ny@happy-science.org
Website: happyscience-usa.org

### New Jersey
66 Hudson St., #2R, Hoboken, NJ 07030, USA
Phone: 1-201-313-0127
Email: nj@happy-science.org
Website: happyscience-usa.org

### Chicago
2300 Barrington Rd., Suite #400,
Hoffman Estates, IL 60169, USA
Phone: 1-630-937-3077
Email: chicago@happy-science.org
Website: happyscience-usa.org

### Florida
5208 8th St., Zephyrhills, FL 33542, USA
Phone: 1-813-715-0000
Fax: 1-813-715-0010
Email: florida@happy-science.org
Website: happyscience-usa.org

### Atlanta
1874 Piedmont Ave., NE Suite 360-C
Atlanta, GA 30324, USA
Phone: 1-404-892-7770
Email: atlanta@happy-science.org
Website: happyscience-usa.org

### San Francisco
525 Clinton St.
Redwood City, CA 94062, USA
Phone & Fax: 1-650-363-2777
Email: sf@happy-science.org
Website: happyscience-usa.org

### Los Angeles
1590 E. Del Mar Blvd., Pasadena, CA
91106, USA
Phone: 1-626-395-7775
Fax: 1-626-395-7776
Email: la@happy-science.org
Website: happyscience-usa.org

### Orange County
16541 Gothard St. Suite 104
Huntington Beach, CA 92647
Phone: 1-714-659-1501
Email: oc@happy-science.org
Website: happyscience-usa.org

### San Diego
7841 Balboa Ave. Suite #202
San Diego, CA 92111, USA
Phone: 1-626-395-7775
Fax: 1-626-395-7776
E-mail: sandiego@happy-science.org
Website: happyscience-usa.org

### Hawaii
Phone: 1-808-591-9772
Fax: 1-808-591-9776
Email: hi@happy-science.org
Website: happyscience-usa.org

### Kauai
3343 Kanakolu Street, Suite 5
Lihue, HI 96766, USA
Phone: 1-808-822-7007
Fax: 1-808-822-6007
Email: kauai-hi@happy-science.org
Website: happyscience-usa.org

## Toronto

845 The Queensway
Etobicoke, ON M8Z 1N6, Canada
Phone: 1-416-901-3747
Email: toronto@happy-science.org
Website: happy-science.ca

## Vancouver

#201-2607 East 49th Avenue,
Vancouver, BC, V5S 1J9, Canada
Phone: 1-604-437-7735
Fax: 1-604-437-7764
Email: vancouver@happy-science.org
Website: happy-science.ca

## INTERNATIONAL

### Tokyo

1-6-7 Togoshi, Shinagawa,
Tokyo, 142-0041, Japan
Phone: 81-3-6384-5770
Fax: 81-3-6384-5776
Email: tokyo@happy-science.org
Website: happy-science.org

### Seoul

74, Sadang-ro 27-gil,
Dongjak-gu, Seoul, Korea
Phone: 82-2-3478-8777
Fax: 82-2-3478-9777
Email: korea@happy-science.org
Website: happyscience-korea.org

### London

3 Margaret St.
London, W1W 8RE United Kingdom
Phone: 44-20-7323-9255
Fax: 44-20-7323-9344
Email: eu@happy-science.org
Website: www.happyscience-uk.org

### Taipei

No. 89, Lane 155, Dunhua N. Road,
Songshan District, Taipei City 105, Taiwan
Phone: 886-2-2719-9377
Fax: 886-2-2719-5570
Email: taiwan@happy-science.org
Website: happyscience-tw.org

### Sydney

516 Pacific Highway, Lane Cove North,
2066 NSW, Australia
Phone: 61-2-9411-2877
Fax: 61-2-9411-2822
Email: sydney@happy-science.org

### Kuala Lumpur

No 22A, Block 2, Jalil Link Jalan Jalil
Jaya 2, Bukit Jalil 57000,
Kuala Lumpur, Malaysia
Phone: 60-3-8998-7877
Fax: 60-3-8998-7977
Email: malaysia@happy-science.org
Website: happyscience.org.my

### Sao Paulo

Rua. Domingos de Morais 1154,
Vila Mariana, Sao Paulo SP
CEP 04010-100, Brazil
Phone: 55-11-5088-3800
Email: sp@happy-science.org
Website: happyscience.com.br

### Kathmandu

Kathmandu Metropolitan City,
Ward No. 15, Ring Road, Kimdol,
Sitapaila Kathmandu, Nepal
Phone: 977-1-427-2931
Email: nepal@happy-science.org

### Jundiai

Rua Congo, 447, Jd. Bonfiglioli
Jundiai-CEP, 13207-340, Brazil
Phone: 55-11-4587-5952
Email: jundiai@happy-science.org

### Kampala

Plot 877 Rubaga Road, Kampala
P.O. Box 34130 Kampala, UGANDA
Phone: 256-79-4682-121
Email: uganda@happy-science.org

# HAPPY SCIENCE UNIVERSITY

## THE FOUNDING SPIRIT AND THE GOAL OF EDUCATION

Based on the founding philosophy of the university, "Exploration of happiness and the creation of a new civilization," education, research and studies will be provided to help students acquire deep understanding grounded in religious belief and advanced expertise with the objectives of producing "great talents of virtue" who can contribute in a broad-ranging way to serve Japan and the international society.

## FACULTIES

**Faculty of human happiness**

Students in this faculty will pursue liberal arts from various perspectives with a multidisciplinary approach, explore and envision an ideal state of human beings and society.

**Faculty of successful management**

This faculty aims to realize successful management that helps organizations to create value and wealth for society and to contribute to the happiness and the development of management and employees as well as society as a whole.

**Faculty of future creation**

Students in this faculty study subjects such as political science, journalism, performing arts and artistic expression, and explore and present new political and cultural models based on truth, goodness and beauty.

**Faculty of future industry**

This faculty aims to nurture engineers who can resolve various issues facing modern civilization from a technological standpoint and contribute to the creation of new industries of the future.

# HAPPY SCIENCE ACADEMY
# JUNIOR AND SENIOR HIGH SCHOOL

Happy Science Academy Junior and Senior High School is a boarding school founded with the goal of educating the future leaders of the world who can have a big vision, persevere, and take on new challenges.

Currently, there are two campuses in Japan; the Nasu Main Campus in Tochigi Prefecture, founded in 2010, and the Kansai Campus in Shiga Prefecture, founded in 2013.

Nasu Main Campus

Kansai Campus

# ABOUT HS PRESS

HS Press is an imprint of IRH Press Co., Ltd. IRH Press Co., Ltd., based in Tokyo, was founded in 1987 as a publishing division of Happy Science. IRH Press publishes religious and spiritual books, journals, magazines and also operates broadcast and film production enterprises. For more information, visit *okawabooks.com*.

*Follow us on:*

f Facebook: Okawa Books     ◎ Instagram: OkawaBooks

▶ Youtube: Okawa Books     🐦 Twitter: Okawa Books

𝓟 Pinterest: Okawa Books     g Goodreads: Ryuho Okawa

———— **NEWSLETTER** ————

To receive book related news, promotions and events, please subscribe to our newsletter below.

🔗 eepurl.com/bsMeJj

 ———— **AUDIO / VISUAL MEDIA** ————

**YOUTUBE**            **PODCAST**

Introduction of Ryuho Okawa's titles; topics ranging from self-help, current affairs, spirituality, religion, and the universe.

# BOOKS BY RYUHO OKAWA

## THE LAWS OF THE SUN
### ONE SOURCE, ONE PLANET, ONE PEOPLE

Paperback • 288 pages • $15.95
ISBN: 978-1-942125-43-3

Imagine if you could ask God why he created this world and what spiritual laws he used to shape us—and everything around us. In *The Laws of the Sun*, Okawa outlines these laws of the universe and provides a road map for living one's life with greater purpose and meaning. This powerful book shows the way to realize true happiness—a happiness that continues from this world through the other.

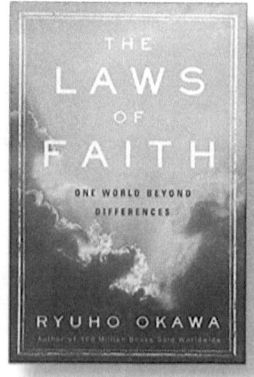

## THE LAWS OF FAITH
### ONE WORLD BEYOND DIFFERENCES

Paperback • 208 pages • $15.95
ISBN: 978-1-942125-34-1

Ryuho Okawa preaches at the core of a new universal religion from various angles while integrating logical and spiritual viewpoints in mind with current world situations. This book offers us the key to accept diversities beyond differences in ethnicity, religion, race, gender, descent, and so on, harmonize the individuals and nations and create a world filled with peace and prosperity.

---

*For a complete list of books, visit okawabooks.com*

# CRITIQUE OF CURRENT WORLD AFFAIRS

### IMMANUEL KANT'S ADVICE FROM HEAVEN

Paperback • 112 pages

"We can clearly see from Kant's message that we constantly need to enlighten people in order to prevent humankind from falling into a dangerous, hellish way of thinking."

-From Preface

[This book is available only in local branches and temples of Happy Science. Please refer to the contact information.]

# THE TRUMP SECRET

### SEEING THROUGH THE PAST, PRESENT, AND FUTURE OF THE NEW AMERICAN PRESIDENT

Paperback • 208 pages • $14.95
ISBN: 978-1-942125-22-8

This book contains a series of lectures and interviews that unveil the secrets to Trump's victory and makes predictions of what will happen under his presidency. This book predicts the coming of a new America that will go through a great transformation from the "red and blue states" to the United States.

---

*For a complete list of books, visit <u>okawabooks.com</u>*

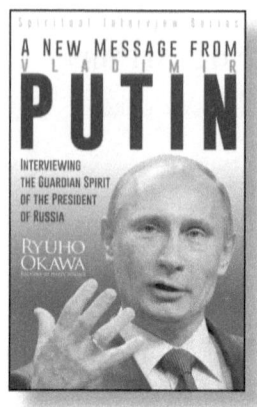

# A NEW MESSAGE FROM VLADIMIR PUTIN

### INVERVIEWING THE GUARDIAN SPIRIT OF THE PRESIDENT OF RUSSIA

Paperback • 232 pages • $14.95
ISBN: 978-1-937673-94-9

We hereby bring you the spiritual message from the guardian spirit of President Putin, the politician who is the center of attention of not just the people of Russia but of the whole world, regardless of it being in a good or a bad way. In the Preface, it says, "President Putin's true intentions, which are 90 percent misunderstood."

# CHINA'S HIDDEN AGENDA

### THE MASTERMIND BEHIND THE ANTI-AMERICAN AND ANTI-JAPANESE PROTESTS

Paperback • 179 pages • $14.95
ISBN: 978-1-937673-18-5

"I wanted to stir up the anti-American movement in the Arab world to make sure that the United States won't be able to attack Syria or Iran...I'm the mastermind behind the Muhammad video."

—Xi Jinping's Guardian Spirit

---